*"To be competitive in today's marketplace
requires a rudimentary understanding
of key finance and accounting concepts."*

"With just a little effort on your part, you can become financially literate."

Finance for Nonfinancial Managers

24 Lessons for Understanding and Evaluating Financial Health

KATHERINE WAGNER

McGraw-Hill

New York Chicago San Francisco Lisbon
London Madrid Mexico City Milan New Delhi
San Juan Seoul Singapore Sydney Toronto

The McGraw·Hill Companies

6 7 8 9 0   DOC/DOC   0 9 8 7

ISBN: 0-07-145090-4

McGraw-Hill books are available at special quantity discounts to use as premi-
ums and sales promotions, or for use in corporate training programs. For more
information, please write to the Director of Special Sales, Professional
Publishing, McGraw-Hill, Two Penn Plaza, New York, NY 10121-2298. Or contact
your local bookstore.

 This book is printed on recycled, acid-free paper containing a minimum
of 50% recycled de-inked fiber.

To order
Finance for
Nonfinancial Managers
call 1-800-842-3075

Contents

☑ *Become finance savvy*

*I*f numbers are the alphabet of the business world, then financial statements and budgets are the books.

To be competitive in today's marketplace requires a rudimentary understanding of key finance and accounting concepts. This book will help give you the financial knowledge you need to succeed at your job.

For many managers, financial statements and budgets are a mystery. If you normally spend your workday planning marketing campaigns or recruiting new employees, you probably don't look forward to preparing your annual budget—or reading through your company's financial statements.

But it doesn't have to be that way.

With just a little effort on your part, you can become financially literate. You may not be able to speak the language of finance fluently, but you can learn it well enough to manage your way around.

The secret to success is that you don't have to learn everything there is to know about finance and accounting. You only need to learn enough to know the right questions to ask.

This book isn't designed to make you into a finance manager or an accountant. Instead, it presents basic information that will help you build your skills. You might want to keep it nearby. It will come in handy whenever you are called on to analyze why your department is over budget or when you want to know how well your company is performing financially.

This book is divided into two sections. The first deals with basic accounting concepts and financial statements. The second half covers the budgeting process.

Although you don't need to read the book in chronological order, it might be helpful to do so, especially if you are unfamiliar with finance and accounting. Although each chapter is designed to stand on its own, certain terms and phrases are introduced in one chapter with subsequent chapters expanding on the topic.

After you read this book, you may find that there are certain topics about which you're interested in learning more. If that's the case, many resources are available. You can buy a book that discusses the topic in more depth or take an evening class at a nearby college.

Remember that this book is the starting point in your journey to evaluating and understanding financial health, not the end point.

✓ *Review basic terms*

*F*or most people, the word *credit* brings to mind a line of credit that you can tap into at some future date or the amount that appears on your bank statement when you make a deposit.

But to accountants, credit has another definition. It's a designation for the right-hand column of the double-ledger accounting system. The left-hand side is known as the debit column. In the double-ledger system, debits and credits must be equal.

It's certainly not necessary—or even recommended—that you learn about or understand the double-ledger system. But it's useful to know that when accountants use a term such as debit or credit they may not be saying what you think they are.

To make sure you're speaking the same language as finance people, here's a list of some commonly used finance and accounting terms:

- *Asset/liability:* An *asset* is an economic resource that a company owns. A *liability* is a resource that the company owes. Land and machinery held by the company are assets, while debt is a liability.
- *Book value/market value: Book value* is the amount of an asset or liability shown on the companies' official financial statements based on the historical, or original, cost. *Market value* is the current value of the asset or liability. In most cases, book value doesn't equal market value.
- *Capital goods:* These are machines and tools used to produce other goods. For many companies, the purchase of capital goods represents a major investment.

- *Depreciation/amortization: Depreciation* is a system that spreads the cost of a tangible asset, such as machinery, over the useful life of the asset. *Amortization* is a system that spreads the cost of an intangible asset, such as a patent, over the useful life of the asset.
- *Fiscal year:* A company's financial reporting year—for example, July 1 to June 30. In most cases the fiscal year is not the same as the calendar year—that is, January 1 to December 31.
- *Profit margin:* This is profit—what the company's owners keep after paying all the bills—as a percentage of sales or revenue.
- *Receivables/payables: Receivables* are money owed to the company, usually for goods and services. *Payables* are money the company owes to others, including suppliers.
- *Revenue/expenses: Revenue* is income that flows into a company. Revenue includes sales, interest, and rents. The terms revenue, sales, and income are often used interchangeably. *Expenses* are costs that are matched to a specific time period, such as by month. Cost is the price paid to acquire an asset.

The preceding list is only a starting point. Follow these suggestions to continue learning:

Ask questions: If you hear people use a term you're not sure about, ask them what it means.

Keep educating yourself: The more you know, the easier it gets. Read business books and publications.

Make your own list: As you come across other terms, jot them in the margins of this chapter so you can refer to them as needed.

The Bottom Line

Improve your business skills by expanding your financial vocabulary.

☐ Make assumptions

☑ *Don't assume*

*F*or people with limited financial background, it's easy to make snap judgments about the information presented in financial statements. In some cases, people make these judgments after only a cursory glance at the numbers and the calculation of a few profit measures.

If you really want to understand financial statements, however, you must be willing to dig deeper than the numbers that appear on the page. While learning some basic accounting concepts will help, just having this knowledge won't make you a savvy financial statement user. To become that, you'll need to be curious and follow up on the numbers you see.

As you read financial statements you might notice an unusual number or trend. Instead of just letting it go at that, it's important to investigate further and ask questions such as the following:

Is this really a trend, or is this a result of some change in accounting procedure? When did this condition start? What's causing it? Is the condition unique to this one company, or is it happening to competitors as well?

For a complete picture of what is going on, you'll need to investigate the company and the industry in which it operates. There are a number of resources to help you, with the most obvious being the company's annual report, which includes all the financial statements as well as additional information about the company's long-term goals.

You'll also want to read business and industry publications, as it's extremely important to understand industry norms and how certain accounting procedures are handled in a given industry.

As an example, imagine that you've inherited a little money and want to invest it in a magazine publisher. You send for the company's annual report and start reading the financial statements.

As you look at the balance sheet—one of the company's official financial statements—you start to have misgivings about investing in the publisher because you notice a large liability balance. Most of this, you note, is caused by deferred income, a term you've never heard before. You're not certain what it is exactly but you assume it can't be good because liabilities are always bad.

As it turns out, however, your assumption about deferred income is wrong. It actually represents prepaid magazine subscriptions and is a source of revenue. Deferred income is common on financial statements in the publishing industry. It appears as a liability because the publisher hasn't earned the income yet by putting out magazines scheduled into the future.

Here are some sources you can contact in your investigations of financial statement information:

Trade associations: Check to see if your local public library has *Gale's Encyclopedia of Associations*. In addition, many trade associations have Web sites.

Accounting societies: They offer information about proposed accounting rule changes that affect a variety of different industry.

Business publishers: There are numerous books that give industry statistics and standards.

The Bottom Line

When in doubt, check it out.

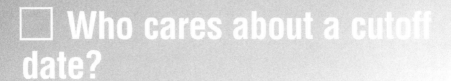

□ Who cares about a cutoff date?

☑ *Understand the importance of timing*

*L*ike most things in life, when it comes to accounting, timing is everything. Timing is especially important when it comes to business transactions and how they are recorded on the financial statements.

Businesses use two types of methods to record transactions: cash and accrual. The cash accounting method records transactions only when money exchanges hands. Accrual accounting, on the other hand, records transactions when the transaction is complete, whether or not the transaction has been paid for yet.

Small businesses often use cash accounting because of its simplicity. For these businesses, revenue is recorded when the customer pays and expenses are recorded when the company pays for them.

However, most large businesses use accrual accounting, which is more complex than the cash basis. The purpose of the accrual method is to match revenues with the expenses that were used to earn them. To accomplish this, transactions are recorded when an economic event has occurred, such as a product being shipped or a machine being repaired, rather than when they are paid.

For example, let's say for the current accounting period Nicko Corporation has booked orders worth $20,000 but actually has collected $10,000 in revenues. The company has expenses of $4,000 for salaries, and it has used inventory valued at $5,000 during the period, although it has only been obligated to pay for $1,000 worth of inventory.

If Nicko Corporation operates on a cash basis, it might look like the example below.

Cash receipts	$10,000
Cash disbursements	
Inventory	1,000
Salaries	4,000
Total disbursements	($5,000)
Excess of receipts over disbursement	$5,000

Now let's see how the same set of facts would look if the company used the accrual method of accounting.

Revenue	$20,000
Expenses	
Inventory	5,000
Salaries	4,000
Total expenses	($9,000)
Net income	$ 11,000

This report gives us more information. For example, it makes it clear how much inventory it took to produce sales of $20,000.

Here are key points to remember about accrual accounting:

Matching principle: The accrual method matches revenues with associated expenses.

Timing: The accrual method records revenue that has been earned but not paid and expenses owed but not paid.

Cash flow: The accrual method does not track cash inflows and outflows.

The Bottom Line

Accrual accounting records transactions when they happen; cash accounting records transactions when cash changes hands.

☐ Who knows what the auditor does?

☑ *Understand what the auditor does*

As you read a company's annual report, you'll notice that it includes an auditor's opinion about the company's financial statements. In many cases, people are confused about the role of the independent auditor.

People often think that it's the auditor's job to verify that the financial statements are accurate. But this isn't the case. It would be extremely difficult for an auditor to be certain that financial statements are accurate unless the auditing firm was responsible for recording the transactions and then preparing the reports. And if that were to happen, the auditor would no longer be independent.

In their capacity as objective outsiders, auditors evaluate whether the financial statements present fairly the company's financial position and the results of its operations and its cash flows. They do this in several ways, including sending out letters to customers, suppliers, and other entities and asking them to confirm financial information that's recorded on the company's books.

Auditors also test internal control procedures. Companies establish controls to minimize the possibility of error and fraud. From the auditor's viewpoint, some of the most important controls are those that involve accounts with access to cash, such as accounts payable.

For example, management may require accounts payable clerks to match a supplier invoice with the receiving record and purchase order so that the company only pays valid supplier invoices. The auditor does testing to determine if accounts payable clerks actually perform the control procedure.

The auditor checks to see if invoices were properly matched with the required documents. The testing is done on a random sample of invoices. Depending on the sample results, the auditor may decide to perform further testing to make sure that any lapses of improperly matching invoices haven't resulted in a material misstatement of accounts payable.

The question of materiality is an important one for auditors. Throughout the audit process, auditors are constantly assessing whether any errors would mislead users of the financial statements.

For instance, if during an audit an auditor uncovers a computer program making rounding errors that end up charging customers a few cents more or a few cents less, the auditor would probably consider this to be immaterial—in other words, inconsequential to the users of financial statements. However, if it turns out that the program's rounding errors have a large cumulative effect, the auditor may decide that the miscalculation is material and ask the company to revise the financial statements.

Here is some additional information about auditors:

Audit opinion: Auditors can give a "clean" opinion or a "qualified" opinion about financial statements.

Internal versus external: Internal auditors are employees of the firm, while external auditors are independent third parties.

Auditor change: A change in auditors by a company could be a red flag, and the situation requires further investigation.

The Bottom Line

Auditors provide an opinion about the financial statements, not a guarantee.

☐ Memorize all the accounting rules

☑ *Learn where to go for answers*

*W*hile it isn't necessary for you to know the rules accountants use to prepare the financial statements, it is important that you understand why the rules exist and where to go to learn more about them.

Just as there are rules regarding how fast you can drive your car on city streets, there are rules about how companies are to report information on the financial statements. One of the main reasons for the rules is to ensure that financial statements are consistent.

This consistency gives financial statement users a better picture of a company's performance over a period of time.

Even when companies follow the rules, there still can be variances on the financial statements, and you need to be aware of these. In some cases, these variances are caused by unusual transactions that are outside the scope of normal operations and not likely to happen again.

An example of this type of variance is the sale of equipment that is no longer being used by the company. Quite often this sales transaction will result in a substantial gain or loss that appears on a financial statement as an extraordinary item. The income statement will also include net income shown both with and without the extraordinary item.

If you are comparing an income statement—one of a company's key financial statements—from a year where there is no extraordinary item with a year that has one, you'll probably want to use the net income before extraordinary income, for comparison purposes. You'll also want to check the footnotes to learn more about the nature of the extraordinary item and the effect it had on the company's financial statements.

One-time occurrences aren't the only events that trigger financial statement variances. Companies also change the methods they use to calculate items such as inventory and depreciation. Choosing a method is sometimes a subjective decision and occasionally there is a need to switch.

If there is a change in accounting methods, there will be a discussion of it in the footnotes. In addition, the accumulated effect caused by the change will appear on the balance sheet, another of a company's key financial statements.

The exact rules and regulations that companies must follow vary from country to country. In the United States, accountants adhere to the rules developed by the Financial Accounting Standards Board (FASB). These rules are known as GAAP, short for Generally Accepted Accounting Principles.

Here are sources you can use to learn more about the rules and regulations governing publicly traded companies:

Annual report: Contact the specific company and ask them for their latest annual report.

U.S. Securities and Exchange Commission (SEC): You can obtain copies of reports that companies are required to file with the SEC.

Business publications: Read up on industry standards and proposed changes.

The Bottom Line

You don't need to know the rules, you just need to know where to find them.

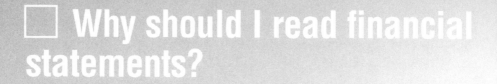

Why should I read financial statements?

Learn the score

*F*inancial statements are the way businesses keep score.

In the sports world, teams keep track of information, including how many games they've won or lost, how many games they've won at home, and how well individual team players are doing.

Financial statements serve the same purpose as sports scorecards. They provide the raw numbers that are needed to create meaningful statistics and ratios to answer questions such as the following: What is the company's most profitable product line? How well has the company used its assets? How efficient has the company been at collecting money from customers?

Once a sports team has calculated statistics for the team and individual players, they use that information in several different ways. First, they compare the current season's numbers to past seasons' numbers to see if the team's performance is getting better or getting worse.

They also compare team statistics against other sports teams so that the numbers will have context. As an example, simply knowing that a professional baseball player has a batting average of .333 doesn't mean much until you compare that average against other pro players.

Financial statements and business statistics work the same way as sports statistics. The information from financial statements is most useful when it is compared with the company's past performance and the performance of other businesses in the same industry.

A variety of people use financial statements to guide business decisions. Potential investors perform calculations to measure profitability before they buy stock. Creditors assess a company's ability to pay its bills before they make a loan. Managers assess how well a new marketing plan is working by analyzing the performance of a product line.

To make these decisions, the users of financial statements need to do more than simply look at the numbers on the page. Making this kind of quick assessment will most likely result in wrong conclusions and faulty decisions.

Financial statements can show those areas of the company that are efficient and those that need to improve. The statements can provide insight into problems the company is having, but to fully understand the situation, you'll need to do additional investigation.

One way to understand financial statements better is to remember the acronym ILE, which stands for:

*I*dentify key numbers.
*L*ook deeper and ask why.
*E*xamine the entire statement.

The following are the three most common financial statements:

Balance sheet: Lists assets, liabilities, and owners' equity, which is the value of the business to the stockholders.

Income statement: Deducts expenses from revenue to arrive at net income, otherwise known as profit.

Statement of cash flow: Shows the sources, uses, and availability of money to the business.

The Bottom Line

As you read financial statements, remember the acronym ILE (identify, look deeper, and examine).

☐ **All I care about is if the balance sheet balances**

☑ *Look closer at the balance sheet*

---

*T*he balance sheet provides a snapshot of the company's financial strength at the end of the accounting period.

The balance sheet gets its name from the fact that it follows a simple equation:

Assets = Liabilities + Owners' or Stockholders' Equity.

Whenever one side of the formula is increased or decreased, the other side must be also.

As an example, if a company buys new equipment on credit, assets are increased to reflect the equipment that the company now owns, while liabilities are increased to reflect the amount the company owes for the purchase.

The assets shown on the balance sheet are divided into current or long-term assets. Current assets are cash or other valuables that are expected to be converted into cash within a year. Typical current assets are cash, accounts receivable, and inventory. Long-term assets include property, plant, and equipment.

Like assets, liabilities are also shown as current and long term. Current liabilities are expected to be paid within a year and include accounts payable and accrued payroll—amounts that employees have earned but have not been paid for yet. Long-term liabilities are typically lease contracts and debt to be repaid over many years.

The owners' equity or stockholders' equity is the owners' value in the business.

Nicko Corporation

Balance Sheet

For the Year Ended June 30

Assets

Total current assets	$50,000
Total long-term assets	5,000
Total assets	$55,000

Liabilities

Total current liabilities	$25,000
Total long-term liabilities	8,000
Total liabilities	$33,000
Stockholders' equity	$22,000
Total liabilities and stockholders' equity	$55,000

As you read through the balance sheet, keep these points in mind:

Accounts receivable: How does the company adjust for customers who are not likely to pay?

Inventory: Is all the inventory sellable?

Long-term debt: Does the current portion due of long-term debt appear under total current liabilities?

The Bottom Line

The balance sheet gives a picture of the financial condition of a company on a given day.

☑ *Read the entire income statement*

*T*he income statement provides the bottom line. Literally. The last line on the statement is net income, which is the amount of revenue that remains after all costs and expenses have been deducted.

The income statement shows the revenues and expenses that occurred over a given period, usually a month, quarter, or year. The statement is sometimes called the profit and loss statement because it provides two measures of profitability, gross profit and net profit, which are also called gross income and net income.

Gross profit is sales revenue less the cost of goods sold, commonly known as COGS. The cost of goods sold includes inventory, labor costs to produce goods, and other costs associated with the production of goods.

Net profit is sales revenue minus all costs and expenses. Net income is usually shown both before and after the effects of income taxes. The net income per share of stock is also shown.

The statement shows gross profit, followed by expenses, which are grouped into categories such as sales and marketing, engineering, research and development, and general and administrative.

To make income statements easier to read, all companies, regardless of size, follow the same format:

Nicko Corporation
Income Statement
For the Year Ended June 30

Sales	$100,000
Cost of goods sold	(30,000)
Gross profit	70,000
Expenses	
Research and development	10,000
General and administrative	40,000
Total expenses	(50,000)
Net profit	$ 20,000

As you read the income statement be on the lookout for the following:

Prior year's numbers: The prior year's numbers are usually shown alongside the most recent.

Unusual items: These are one-time events such as the profit or loss from the disposal of a business.

Gross loss or net loss instead of profit: These will require further research to find out why.

The Bottom Line

The income statement shows the profit for a given period.

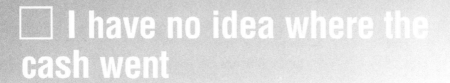

☐ I have no idea where the cash went

☑ *Check the cash flow*

Most people are familiar with the balance sheet and income statement but less so with the cash flow statement. In some ways, the cash flow statement might be the most important of the three. Companies can remain in business without turning a profit but they won't last for long with a negative cash flow.

When many people hear the term cash flow statement they assume the report shows cash coming in and going out, much the same way you record deposits and checks in your checkbook. While this method does display money flowing in and out of the business, it fails to show how net income relates to net cash flow.

The cash flow statement starts with net income and then goes through a series of adjustments to reconcile the net income to net cash flow. The exact method for making these adjustments is quite complex and requires a thorough understanding of how various account balances affect cash.

The adjustments are then divided into three groups: operations, investing, and financing. Here is a simplified version of a cash flow statement that shows some of the key parts of the report:

Cash Flow Statement

For the Year Ended December 31

Operations

Net income	$100,000
Add back depreciation, since no cash is used	5,000
Cash flow provided by operations	105,000

Investing activities

Purchase of office equipment	(10,000)
Cash flow used by investing activities	(10,000)

Financing activities

Borrowing from bank	15,000
Cash flow provided by financing activities	15,000
Net cash flow	110,000
Add beginning cash balance	15,000
Ending cash balance	$125,000

Understanding the cash flow statement can be tricky. Here are some tips to help:

Follow the numbers: The items on the cash flow statement all come from other financial statements.

Purpose of the statement: The cash flow statement serves as an analytical tool.

Don't sweat it: You don't have to understand the adjustments. Just check the right-hand column on the statement to see the net effect.

The Bottom Line

The cash flow statement is a tool that companies use to manage funds on hand.

☐ Skip the footnotes

☑ *Take a closer look at the footnotes*

Don't make the mistake that many people do of ignoring the notes to the financial statements. One of the cardinal rules to understanding financial statements is to read the accompanying footnotes. They're a valuable resource that shouldn't be overlooked.

One of the reasons why footnotes are so crucial is that information on financial statements is usually presented in a summarized format. While this makes the reports easier to read, they often lack detailed explanations of vital points. In addition, there is no place on the financial statements for disclosure of pending lawsuits that could have an impact on future operations.

The footnotes also serve as a place where difficult or complex accounting transactions can be explained. In the course of preparing financial statements management is often asked to make a subjective decision about the treatment of certain transactions, and the results of these decisions are included in the footnotes.

In some cases, footnotes provide a breakdown of numbers that appear on the financial statements, such as expenses or liabilities. As an example, long-term notes payable is recorded as one consolidated amount on the balance sheet. However, since repayment of debt can affect cash flows, it's important for users of financial statements to know the timing of future payments. The answer to the timing question can be found in the footnotes, which provide a debt repayment schedule that lists when amounts are due.

In other cases, such as a lawsuit that has been filed against the company, the footnotes take on a narrative explanation and describe the situation. Each note usually includes the action that instigated the litigation and legal counsel's opinion regarding the potential risk exposure to the company.

One of the most important sections of the footnotes is the company's disclosure of significant accounting policies and practices. Typical information would include the type of inventory method the company uses and the methods the company uses to allocate the costs of assets over their useful lives. There also would be a discussion of how the company treats foreign currency and financial instruments.

Other sections in the footnotes provide detailed information about long-term debt, lease commitments, and income taxes. The footnotes also cover pension plans and other retirement programs, providing information about the program costs and the level of funding.

In addition, the notes include information on stock options granted to employees and officers and discuss how the stock-based compensation was calculated.

As you read through financial statements, keep the footnotes close at hand to use as a reference. Here are highlights of what the footnotes offer:

Significant accounting policies and practices: Supplies information about inventory, depreciation, and amortization policies.

Expense detail: Gives a breakdown of advertising, promotion, and research and development expenses.

Activities affecting future cash flows: Provides payment schedules for long-term debt, leases, and income taxes.

The Bottom Line

Make footnotes required reading.

☐ **Lots of inventory must be good**

☑ *Determine if inventory is too high*

*F*or most companies, inventory is the lifeblood of financial health. After all, if there are no goods to sell, an organization can't stay in business for long.

Since inventory is so vital to a company's continued existence, it follows that the more inventory there is, the better it is. Unfortunately, this isn't always the case.

A large inventory can mean that the company is overproducing goods and not using resources wisely, and it can also mean that the inventory balance includes goods that will never be able to be sold. To determine if this is the case, you'll need to do some investigating.

You'll want to start by checking the footnotes to learn about the company's inventory policy. A change in the method of valuing inventory is a red flag, as it could indicate a problem with the ending balance.

Inventory is goods that are held for sale in the ordinary course of business. For a retail establishment, inventory includes items held in stock. For a manufacturer, inventory includes raw materials, goods in process, and finished goods. Since it costs money to store goods, companies strive to keep inventories at optimal levels, that is, the least amount of goods that can meet customer demand.

At the end of the fiscal year, companies record the inventory they have on hand. There are a number of ways that a company can use to value inventory, including last in, first out (LIFO) and first in, first out (FIFO) methods. The type of product and industry norms influences the valuation method that a company chooses.

As a general rule, once a company selects a method, there must be extraordinary circumstances to switch. If a company changes the valuation method, the reasons should be in the footnotes.

Ideally, goods that have no resale value should be written off at the end of the year and not included in the ending balance. This can include items that have become obsolete, soiled, or damaged. An unusually high inventory balance may mean that these goods have not been taken off the books and are improperly recorded.

Another way to spot problems is to calculate inventory turnover, that is, how many times inventory is sold and replaced with new inventory. This ratio is determined by dividing the cost of goods sold listed on the income statement by the inventory balance. A higher ratio means the goods are turning over more quickly and there is less inventory. As a rule of thumb, a higher ratio is more desirable.

Here are some tips to help you check the accuracy of the inventory balance:

Track inventory levels to sales: Compare inventory balances to sales amounts for the current year and prior years. Investigate if sales have remained steady but inventory levels have increased.

Determine inventory turnover: Be sure to check the ratio to industry standards.

Review industry publications: Make sure that the products the company sells haven't become outdated.

The Bottom Line

Too much inventory may signal future losses.

☑ *Look at adjustments*

*W*hen you evaluate financial statements, you'll want to take some time to review accounts receivable. It's important to verify that it accurately reflects the money the company can reasonably expect to collect from customers rather than the total amount of money that is owed.

When goods are sold to a customer, the seller records the transaction by increasing both the sales and accounts receivable accounts. The invoice amount remains in accounts receivable until either the invoice is paid or it becomes apparent to management that the amount is uncollectible and should be written off, in other words, subtracted from the financial statements as money coming into the company.

At the time of a sale, a company can't know for certain if a particular invoice will be paid or not. In addition, it can be months, or even years, before an uncollectible invoice is written off. This lag time can result in a misstatement of accounts receivable until the invoice amount is taken off the books. The situation will also cause income to be overstated at the time of the initial sale and understated at the time the invoice is written off.

To prevent the misstatement of income and accounts receivable, accountants use a reserve account known as allowance for bad debts or allowance for doubtful accounts. This reserve offsets accounts receivable and decreases net income. The allowance for doubtful accounts is usually a certain percentage of accounts receivable and is adjusted at the end of an accounting period.

Because of the effect that accounts receivable write-offs can have on net income, companies sometimes underestimate their uncollectibles. One way to check for this problem is to compare the current and prior years' sales and accounts receivable balances. The accounts receivable balance should follow the sales trend. For instance, if sales increase slightly, accounts receivable should show moderate gains as well. If accounts receivable is much higher, then it might be overstated.

Another way to spot inflated accounts receivable is to calculate the accounts receivable turnover. To do this, simply divide sales by accounts receivable (Sales/Accounts Receivable). This number shows how many times a year the company collected all its accounts receivable from customers. In general, the higher the number the better.

Once you have the turnover ratio, you can determine the average number of days it takes to collect payments by dividing 365 by the turnover ratio (365/Accounts Receivable Ratio). Companies usually strive to collect payments in 30 days, so 30 is a benchmark. If the collection period is much greater, the company could be having problems collecting money or could be failing to adjust accounts receivable for invoices that will never be paid.

Here are some tips to follow as you check accounts receivable:

Calculate turnover: Compare current and prior years' ratios.

Create a benchmark: Check competitors to determine industry norms for accounts receivable turnover.

Delve deeper: Document the company's credit and collection policies.

The Bottom Line

Be sure a company writes off uncollectibles promptly.

☐ Don't worry when a sale happened

☑ *Check revenue recognition*

*R*evenue is one of the key elements on financial statements. Managers are often under intense pressure to meet quarterly or yearly sales goals. Reaching these goals has a positive impact on the company since it makes shareholders happy, increases employee bonuses, and extends lines of credit.

Because so much is riding on revenue—that is, sales—managers have been known to fudge the numbers in order to make them appear better than they are. In fact, improper recognition of revenue is the most common reason why companies restate earnings on financial statements that have already been published and filed with government regulatory agencies.

While most companies adhere to required guidelines for recognizing revenue, sales is one area of the financial statement you should carefully scrutinize. By becoming knowledgeable about how companies can inflate revenue, you can look for the warning signs.

Revenue is recorded whenever a sale takes place. This happens when ownership of property is transferred or a service is rendered. In some cases, this transfer occurs when goods are shipped from the seller, and in other cases the transfer occurs when the item is delivered to the customer. The invoice or contract will specify the terms of the transfer.

When companies prepare an income statement, the sales figure should reflect all the sales transactions that took place during the specified period. As the quarter- or year-end cut-off date approaches, companies often try to boost the sales numbers. Activity in the shipping department may increase as workers put in longer hours to fill all the orders on file before the end of the month.

However, if these last-minute efforts fall short of the goal, managers sometimes inflate the numbers. They can do this by including sales transactions that aren't completed. Of course, this action only serves to reduce sales in the next period and possibly cause even more revenue manipulation in the future to meet goals.

Accounts receivable may hold clues to improper revenue recognition. Since sales transactions increase both sales and accounts receivable, an inflated sales number will also have a corresponding inflated accounts receivable number.

You might be able to spot this situation by calculating the accounts receivable turnover and accounts receivable period discussed previously. If transactions are recorded too soon, there will be a long wait before customers pay their invoices. This will be reflected in a slow turnover and a long collection period.

To ensure that sales are recorded properly, look at the following:

Treatment of long-term contracts: How much income from long-term contracts is recorded in the current year?

Recording current sales revenue in future periods: Management might record current sales revenue in future periods to smooth out uneven sales numbers. To spot this activity, look for rapid accounts receivable turnover and a quick collection period.

Revenue recognition policy: What are the company procedures?

The Bottom Line

Remember to verify that sales are recorded when they happen.

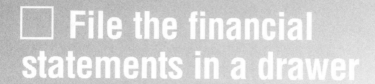

☐ **File the financial statements in a drawer**

☑ *Analyze, analyze, analyze*

*F*inancial statements are more than just a number-crunching exercise. They are important management tools. However, to get the full value of the statements, you'll need to do a little number crunching.

Simply reading the numbers on the statements isn't enough. To understand what the numbers are saying, you need to put them into context; one way to do this is to compare the most recent year's numbers to the prior year's.

The easiest starting point for this type of analysis is with a comparative income statement that puts the numbers side by side:

	Most recent statement	Prior year
Net sales	$120,000	$100,000
Cost of goods sold	(27,000)	(30,000)
Gross profit	$93,000	$70,000
Selling expenses	6,000	5,000
Administrative expenses	45,000	25,000
Total expenses	$51,000	$30,000
Net income	$42,000	$40,000

As you look at the statement above, you'll want to note numbers that increased or decreased dramatically. Then, you'll want to analyze the statements to find relationships that explain why the numbers changed.

Looking at the statement above, you see that net sales increased by $20,000, or 20%, at the same time expenses rose $1,000, for an increase of 20% as well.

Although sales increased by 20%, the cost of the goods sold decreased by $3,000, or 10%. What could account for that change? If you look at administrative expenses, you see an increase of $20,000, or 80%. Is there a connection between the two?

Unfortunately, this condensed format doesn't show a breakdown within the expenses, but if it did, it would show an increase in salaries of $20,000. As it turns out, the company hired a buyer who was able to procure better prices from suppliers.

The same type of analysis can also be performed for the balance sheet and retained earnings statement. To accomplish it, you would use a comparative format to show the most recent year's numbers and prior year's numbers. You would then note any numbers that had a large increase or decrease and look for the underlying cause.

Here are some suggestions to help with financial statement analysis:

Compare to competitors: Perform a comparative analysis in which you compare the most recent numbers to industry averages.

Consider alternatives: Don't just accept the first possible answer to a question.

Keep digging: If you don't find an answer right away, keep looking for it.

The Bottom Line

It pays to critically examine the financial statements.

☐ Use lots of ratios

☑ *Use key ratios*

*A*fter you finish reading the financial statements, you might be thinking: "So what do these numbers mean? Can the company pay its bills? How profitable is it?"

To find answers to those questions, you can use the numbers from the financial statements to create ratios that measure financial condition and profitability. Potential investors, bankers, and management all use measures to assess a company's performance as well as its financial strengths and weaknesses.

There are ratios to measure just about anything. The right ratios to use are those that give you the information you want to know. For instance, you might choose to focus on measures that show company growth or how efficiently it's handling assets and liabilities.

Perhaps the most commonly used measure is the price-to-earnings ratio, also known as the P/E ratio. The ratio is calculated by dividing the market price of a stock by the earnings per share. The resulting number shows the relationship between the price of a stock and the earnings that share of stock will generate for an investor. The number also shows the return that stockholders have received on their investments. This number, however, doesn't mean much by itself and must be compared to the P/E ratio of other companies.

In addition to the P/E ratio, here are four other common measures:

- *Current ratio:* Current Assets/Current Liabilities. This measure is displayed in the form of 3:1. This tells you how well the company could generate cash by selling assets to pay off debt. At first thought, it would seem that a ratio of 1:1 would be adequate, but companies strive for more than a one-to-one ratio because of potential time delays in receiving payments. In general, companies strive for a ratio of 2:1.

- *Quick ratio:* Cash + Accounts Receivable/Current Liabilities. This measure is displayed as 1.4:1. The ratio is similar to the current ratio except that it excludes inventory from the calculation because of problems that can arise in selling inventory, such as spoilage and obsolescence. There is no golden number here, as it varies from industry to industry.
- *Gross profit margin:* Gross Profit/Gross Sales. This number is shown as a percentage, such as 15%. This percentage shows the profit a company makes on what it sells, after the cost to produce the product is deducted but before other costs such as general and administration are deducted.
- *Net profit margin:* Net Profit/Gross Sales. Like the gross profit margin, the net profit margin is shown as a percentage, such as 2%. The net profit margin shows the profit a company makes on the products it sells after all costs are deducted.

Regardless of the measures you are using, here are guidelines you can follow to understand the numbers better:

Watch over time: Don't just do the measure once and forget about it.

Compare against industry standards: Set a benchmark.

Perform measures on each product line: This can pinpoint the more profitable cost centers.

The Bottom Line

Financial measurements are the report cards of the business world.

Why do I need to know about PPE?

☑ *Why PPE is important*

Property, plant, and equipment (PPE), also known as fixed assets, are the physical assets that companies own and use in the course of doing business, including cars, lathes, factories, and undeveloped land. Because these assets require large capital investments, the way their costs are expensed can have a significant impact on the net income.

PPE are considered long-term assets, as they are expected to last for more than a year. However, as machines and equipment are used, their value to the company decreases. This decrease in value is represented by depreciation, which serves to spread the cost of the asset over its working life.

PPE are depreciated over a number of years, because if they were written off in the year of purchase they would create an unrealistic net income for that year as well as those years when the equipment is operating. To understand how this happens, consider the following example:

Nicko Corporation has decided to replace a widget-making machine with a new one. The machine will cost $50,000 and is expected to produce widgets for five years. Nicko's income in the year of the purchase was $200,000 and the following year it was $250,000.

Now, let's see the effect of the equipment purchase on expenses for years 1 and 2. If the entire machine were written off in year 1, it would affect net income as follows:

	Year 1	Year 2
Sales	$200,000	$250,000
Widget machine	(50,000)	——
Net income	$150,000	$250,000

Expensing the entire cost of the machine in the first year misrepresents net income for both years and has made it seem that the machine was totally used up in year 1 and not used in year 2.

Now, look at what happens if Nicko uses straight-line depreciation, a method that spreads the cost of the machine over a five-year life.

	Year 1	Year 2
Sales	$200,000	$250,000
Widget machine	——	——
Depreciation	(10,000)	(10,000)
Net income	$190,000	$240,000

In this second scenario, depreciation expense in years 1 and 2 has decreased net income for both years, thus serving to match income with the expenses necessary to generate it. The $10,000 depreciation expense would continue to be written off against sales in years 3 through 5.

Here are some additional facts about assets:

Balance sheet: PPE appears as a long-term asset on the balance sheet net of the depreciation that has accumulated over the years.

Footnotes: The footnotes provide a thorough breakdown of the assets that are part of PPE.

Expensed immediately: As a rule, small, inexpensive assets are accounted for in the year in which they are purchased because it would be impractical to track such items over a number of years.

The Bottom Line

Depreciation allocates the cost of equipment over its useful life.

☑ *Find out more about goodwill*

Goodwill doesn't appear on all financial statements, but when it does, it's worth understanding how it got there.

When most people hear the word *goodwill* mentioned in relation to business, they think of an intangible asset that arises from the reputation of a business in relation to its customers.

Accountants, however, have a slightly different definition of goodwill. When it appears on the financial statements, it does refer to intangible assets but it doesn't relate to the reputation or operations of the company issuing the financial statements. Instead, it describes the excess price the company paid over fair market value for another firm. The amount of goodwill shown on the balance sheet is that difference.

As an example of how goodwill comes about, let's imagine a scenario where Nicko Corporation wants to purchase Caffe d'Oro, a privately held coffee bean roaster. At the time of the sale, Caffe d'Oro had assets of $400,000, liabilities of $300,000.

Nicko and Caffe d'Oro went through intense negotiations before finally settling on a purchase price of $500,000. As part of the deal, Nicko agreed to assume all Caffe d'Oro's liabilities.

A rundown of the numbers after the sale looks like this:

Assets	$400,000
Liabilities	$300,000
Goodwill	$400,000

The goodwill reflects the difference between the purchase price of $500,000 and the coffee company's book value of $100,000 (assets minus liabilities).

There could be a number of reasons why Nicko was willing to pay a $400,000 premium for Caffe d'Oro. Perhaps the coffee company had an asset that couldn't be shown on paper, such as a loyal customer base or an innovative method for selling coffee. Either way, Nicko thought enough of Caffe d'Oro's operation and reputation to pay more than the company was worth on paper.

Nicko's books would include entries for Caffe d'Oro's assets and liabilities as well as the $400,000 goodwill.

Here is some additional information about goodwill:

Combined financial statements: Once the sale is complete, the buyer combines the financial statements of both companies.

Changing rules: Until 2002, U.S companies were able to amortize goodwill—that is, spread out the expense—over 40 years. Now companies must test the fair value of goodwill and account for the expense when the fair value decreases.

Check the company's reevaluation policy: Writing off goodwill lowers profits for that year, so companies may hesitate to write off goodwill even when the value has decreased.

The Bottom Line

Goodwill is created when one company acquires another and remains on the books until the fair value in the marketplace decreases.

☐ Do the budget on the fly

☑ *Prepare, prepare, prepare*

While there's no magic formula you can use to make budget numbers appear out of thin air, there are a number of steps you can take to make the process run more smoothly. The key is to enlist the help of others who have relevant knowledge.

In some cases, a good starting point is talking to an accountant who is familiar with your industry and company. You might even want to prepare a list of questions beforehand so you don't skip any key points. If the answer to any of your questions is too technical, ask for clarification.

During this phase of the process, you'll also want to share information with other departmental managers. This is the time to find out if there are upcoming projects that may require resources from your department. You also should investigate if there are any untapped resources in the firm that could help reduce expenditures under your control.

Be sure not to overlook the people who report to you. They may know about malfunctioning equipment or machinery that will need to be repaired or replaced in the near future. However, they may be reluctant to share this type of bad news, so you'll have to ask questions that guide them to offer this information.

As an example, you don't want to ask, "Are all the machines working OK?" Instead, ask an open-ended question such as "What types of problems have you had with the machines?" The answer may indicate that you'll need to do further research and budget funds for costly repairs or replacement of equipment.

As you move along in the process, you'll want to refer to the prior year's budget. Don't take those numbers and mark them up. The previous budget should only serve as a guide. While it can be useful, it most likely contains outdated information on which you shouldn't rely.

The previous budgets can help you learn where your strengths and weaknesses are when it comes to budgeting. Look at the budgeted and actual amounts to see which areas had the smallest differences, also known as variances, and which had the largest. Try to figure out how you can improve the process and make your forecasts more accurate.

In addition to the previous suggestions, here are some tips to help the budgeting process:

Allow enough time: It can take two or three months to gather all the information you need.

Start with revenue: Set sales goals and then determine the resources it will take to meet the goals.

Avoid guesstimates: Back up your figures as much as possible.

The Bottom Line

Use the previous budgets as a jumping-off point, not a solution.

☐ Set ambitious sales goals

☑ Set realistic sales goals

Sales forecasting for the annual budget is all about creating balance. While you want to set a sales goal that pushes employees to do their best, you also need to make sure the goal is attainable.

Setting an attainable goal is especially important, because many cash flow decisions are based on projected sales. If sales are expected to rise, management may decide to invest in new equipment or hire new employees. If the sales goal isn't met, however, the company could experience severe cash flow problems.

To make the sales forecast as accurate as possible, you need to allow yourself enough time to gather relevant information and evaluate what it's telling you.

One way to start the process is to ensure that your sales forecast matches company goals and objectives. If management wants to open an overseas office, you'd want to incorporate that goal into the forecast. You might not want to project large increases in domestic sales if the sales staff will be focused on foreign markets. In general, it's a good idea to separate sales forecasts based on factors such as product line or geographic location.

Once you've aligned your evaluation with company goals, you can review historical sales. This information can serve as a guide for analyzing how different factors, such as competitor actions or advertising campaigns, affect sales.

As an example, historical data may suggest that lowering the product price increases sales. So decreasing product price might sound appealing until further investigation reveals that lowering the price also decreases net profits. The best pricing strategy isn't about simply increasing sales, it's also about maximizing profit.

Part of the sales history analysis should focus on the effect of repeat business. Based on past history, how much business from existing customers can you expect in the future? How many long-term contracts and confirmed orders do you have already for the coming year?

An important consideration in many industries is seasonal sales and special promotions. Most businesses don't have steady sales throughout the year, and in many cases these fluctuations follow a predictable pattern.

The budget should reflect varying sales volumes. It may take a little more time to forecast sales for each month but this method is preferable to simply taking the projected total sales and dividing it by 12. This creates an unrealistic sales budget and makes it more difficult to compare budgeted amounts to actual results.

Assess expected future sales by taking the following action:

Scope out the competition: Learn about changes in your competitor's sales strategy.

Read industry publications: Keep up on the latest information.

Check for upcoming special events: Will there be any major one-time events that could affect your sales?

The Bottom Line

Strive for a sales goal that's aggressive and achievable.

☑ *Make judicious cuts*

*Y*ou've crunched them and you've tweaked them. You've spent weeks slaving over the budget numbers and you've finally gotten them right. After all that work, it's no wonder you feel a sense of relief when you hand the budget in.

But just when you thought the process was over, you hear the bad news. Management needs you to go back over the numbers and cut your budget costs by 10%.

You've squeezed every last penny from your budget already, so how can you reduce it even further?

At this point, you might be tempted to simply cut 10% from all your costs, regardless of how feasible it is to reach those goals. You rationalize that this method is the only fair way to do it, since it will require everyone to cut back equally. And, since it doesn't take long to cut everything by 10%, you can make the changes effortlessly and get back to your regular tasks.

On the face of it cutting 10% across the board may solve your problem in the short term, but in the long term it will cause you more headaches. Your job as a manager isn't to find an easy and quick solution to developing a budget. Your responsibility is to create a realistic budget that can serve as a guideline throughout the year. This means that you need to recheck your numbers and find where you can cut back.

As you review your budget, make sure that every line item supports company goals. Those expenditures that don't match can be trimmed. As an example, if management wants to hold the line on hiring in the coming year, you can reduce or eliminate budgeted expenditures for promotional activities aimed at recruiting new employees.

If your budget includes purchasing new equipment or machinery, you might want to consider renting or leasing instead. These types of arrangements can give you access to state-of-the-art equipment while freeing up cash.

You also can investigate alternatives to purchasing. For instance, if your company manufactures goods at a customer's facility, the customer might be willing to buy the equipment and lease it back to you.

For those items that you must purchase, find out if you can negotiate a better price or better terms with a supplier. In some cases, if you sign a long-term contract you can realize significant savings.

Sometimes small cutbacks can add up to big savings, so don't overlook the following:

Shop around for low-price suppliers: Be careful to weigh any price savings against the possible loss of value-added services such as good customer service.

Consider buying used machinery: Rebuilt or reconditioned equipment can cost less than new equipment and work just as well.

Reduce labor costs: Make your department more efficient by replacing time-consuming paperwork with computerized systems.

The Bottom Line

Cutting costs is not an exact science; it may take several rounds to get it right.

☑ *Track cash flow*

A cash budget is an indispensable tool for managing cash flow, that is, whether or not there will be money on hand to meet expenses that are due to be paid. It can help guide decisions such as choosing to lease rather than buy equipment or offering promotions to get customers to pay more quickly.

The cash budget focuses on money that flows in and out of the business. The only transactions that are included are those that increase or decrease the cash balance. This differs from a regular budget, which includes items that don't affect cash, such as credit sales and depreciation of assets.

A cash budget needs to reflect the difference in timing between the sales transaction and the payment of the invoice. For companies that sell on credit, cash inflow is delayed until the customer actually pays. Retailers that deal with cash are at an advantage in terms of anticipating cash inflow over companies that must wait for payment.

The outflow side of the cash budget works much the same way as the inflow. The budget should only include expenditures at the time they are paid. Recurring expenses such as rent and salaries are easy to budget since they occur at regular intervals. It's more difficult to anticipate emergency cash payments so you might want to include a reserve for such cases.

The following example illustrates a simple quarterly cash budget:

Month	October	November	December
Cash, beginning balance	$100,000	$ 85,000	$ 88,000
Cash collections	50,000	35,000	14,000
Total cash available	$150,000	$120,000	$102,000
Cash disbursement for month:			
Salaries	10,000	10,000	10,000
Rent	2,000	2,000	2,000
Payments to suppliers	53,000	20,000	10,000
Total disbursements	(65,000)	(32,000)	(22,000)
Cash on hand at end of month	$ 85,000	$ 88,000	$ 80,000

The cash budget can often pinpoint a potential problem with cash flow. If that's the case, the company can hold the line on purchases and buy only essential items. In addition, they can ask for extended payment terms from suppliers. However, certain expenditures, such as salaries, are often the largest cash outflows and the most difficult to delay paying.

Follow these steps as you prepare your cash budget:

Include short-term bank loan proceeds and associated repayments: These items don't appear on the balance sheet or income statement but belong in a cash budget.

Update on a monthly basis: Be certain you have enough cash to cover your upcoming disbursements.

Anticipate repairs: If you have old equipment or machinery, be sure to budget for service calls.

The Bottom Line

Monitoring cash flow can be the difference between staying in business or going broke.

☑ *Spot potential problems*

*T*he purpose of a budget isn't to give managers headaches. In fact, a budget can be a manager's friend. Budgets are useful control tools that can help managers analyze the difference between expected activity and actual results.

A budget variance analysis—identifying where actual results differ from budgeted estimates—helps managers pinpoint areas where the company is having trouble meeting goals.

To perform the analysis, you need to look at the budget and the actual number side by side, making a note of the variance between the two. Rather than trying to keep track of whether a variance is negative or positive, you may find it easier to record whether actual results are favorable or unfavorable compared to the budget.

The following is a simplified version of a budget report showing actual and budget amounts for the month of July for Nicko Corporation:

	Actual	Budget	Variance	Favorable/ Unfavorable
Month	July	July		
Number of widgets sold	100,000	125,000	25,000	U
Sales total	$300,000	$375,000	$75,000	U
Cost of goods sold	(150,000)	(155,000)	(5,000)	F
Gross profit	$150,000	$220,000	$70,000	U

	Actual	Budget	Variance	Favorable/ Unfavorable
Expenses				
Advertising	$5,000	$15,000	$10,000	F
Salaries	55,000	55,000	0	
Telephone	2,000	5,000	3,000	F
Depreciation	3,000	3,000	0	
Total expenses	65,000	78,000	13,000	F
Net income	$85,000	$142,000	$57,000	U

An analysis of key numbers will show why it's important to investigate what the numbers are telling you.

At first glance, it looks as though Nicko failed to reach its sales goal and managed to reduce projected advertising and telephone expenses. This isn't the case, however.

Managers at Nicko had projected sales of $375,000 based on a promotion that was supposed to begin the first week of July. But there was a delay, and the special didn't go into effect until August. In addition, Nicko had budgeted additional telephone expenses that might arise in relation to the promotion.

Since this is the second time that a promotion has been canceled, managers at Nicko will want to investigate the situation further.

Incorporate the following steps into your budget analysis:

Don't dwell on the numbers: Find the underlying reasons.

Incorporate percentages: Construct another column that shows percentage variance, calculated by dividing variance by the budget (Variance/Budget). This makes the report easier to read.

Use your time wisely: Only follow up on those variances that are significant.

The Bottom Line

Budget analysis lets you know where you need to take action.

☐ Aren't all costs the same?

☑ *Understand how sales affect costs*

When preparing your budget, keep in mind that not all costs are created equally. While fixed costs remain the same regardless of the sales volume, variable costs go up or down with sales.

By understanding the relationship between costs and sales, you have a tool to help you make reasonable predictions about your department's spending.

Fixed costs are expenditures that stay the same over a period of time. Examples of fixed costs include rent, scheduled maintenance and repairs, staff salaries, accounting fees, and depreciation of fixed assets.

Whether you sell one widget or a million widgets, the fixed costs will be steady.

On the other hand, variable costs rise and fall with your sales. The more widgets you sell, the higher your variable costs will go. Typical variable costs include raw materials, overtime pay, and wages linked directly to output.

As an example, Nicko Corporation sells widgets at $10 each. The weekly fixed costs for Nicko Corporation are $500 and the variable costs are $2 per widget. If, during the first week of operation the company sells 100 widgets, it will have sales of $1,000, fixed costs of $500, and variable costs of $200.

Now, let's suppose that in the second week Nicko Corporation sells 200 widgets. In this case, it has sales of $2,000, fixed costs of $500, and variable costs of $400.

For either week, Nicko Corporation had fixed costs of $500, but its variable costs rose by $200, with the additional 100 units sold in the second week. In this case, Nicko's total costs for the first week were $700 and for the second week $900.

Week	Number of Widgets Sold	Sales Revenue	Fixed Costs	Variable Costs	Total Costs
1	100	$1,000	$500	$200	$700
2	200	$2,000	$500	$400	$900

Like the Nicko Corporation, you'll want to understand which costs are linked to your sales function. You can then plug in the variable expenditure based on the sales projection.

Here's a strategy to help you sort fixed costs from variable costs:

First step: Create a list of all your costs.

Second step: Analyze how the costs relate to sales.

Third step: Group your costs into fixed amounts or into those that relate to sales.

The Bottom Line

Variable costs increase and decrease with the sales volume.

☑ *Select the right type of budget*

*F*lexible budgeting doesn't mean that you can pick and choose when you do the budget. But it does refer to a budget that accommodates a variety of activity levels.

For companies with a range of sales volume and variable costs, flexible budgets may be a better choice than fixed budgets, which don't change projected costs to reflect differing sales volumes. Flexible budgets make it easier for managers to be accountable for variances in costs that they control.

The flexible budget begins with an analysis of fixed costs such as rent and salaries. These items will remain the same, regardless of the projected sales. The next step is to find out the relationship that the variable costs have to sales.

Let's walk through an example of how a company goes about putting a flexible budget together. Nicko Corporation, a manufacturer that produces widgets, has projected that sales for the month of July could come in at three different levels: 100,000, 250,000 and 300,000. Nicko sells the widgets for $2 apiece.

Nicko then rents factory space for $15,000 a month and has a monthly payroll of $100,000. Nicko's full-time workers are able to produce 100,000 widgets a month. For every 50,000 more widgets Nicko needs to produce a month, the company must pay overtime of $5,000. In addition, raw materials needed to produce 100,000 widgets costs Nicko $30,000.

Here is how the above information would look in a flexible budget format:

Sales volume	100,000	250,000	300,000
Revenue	$200,000	$500,000	$600,000
Fixed costs			
Rent			
Salaries	$115,000	$115,000	$115,000
Variable costs			
Overtime			
Raw materials	$30,000	$90,000	$110,000

At the end of July, managers at Nicko compared budgeted numbers to actual:

	Actual	Budget	Variance	Favorable/ Unfavorable
Widgets produced	250,000	250,000		
Fixed costs	$117,000	$115,000	$2,000	U
Variable costs	$105,000	$90,000	$15,000	U

There could be many reasons why the variable costs were higher than the budgeted amounts. At this point, the managers at Nicko would want to investigate the underlying cause of the variance.

The following tips will help you prepare your flexible budget:

Find relationships: You'll need to figure out how variable expenses relate to sales.

Use a formula: If possible, create a formula that calculates variable expenses based on sales volume.

Review the flexible budget regularly: Keep sharpening the saw.

The Bottom Line

A flexible budget is a good choice for companies that have different levels of sales activity.

*"If you don't find an answer right away,
keep looking for it."*

The McGraw-Hill Professional Education Series

How to Manage Performance: 24 Lessons for Improving Performance

By Robert Bacal (0-07-143531-X)

Goal-focused, commonsense techniques for stimulating greater productivity in the workplace and fostering true commitment.

Dealing with Difficult People: 24 Lessons for Bringing Out the Best in Everyone

By Rick Brinkman and Rick Kirschner (0-07-141641-2)

Learn about the 10 types of problem people and how to effectively respond to them to improve communication and collaboration.

How to Motivate Every Employee: 24 Proven Tactics to Spark Productivity in the Workplace

By Anne Bruce (0-07-141333-2)

By a master motivator and speaker, this book quickly reviews practical ways you can turn on employees and enhance their performance and your own.

Six Sigma for Managers: 24 Lessons to Understand and Apply Six Sigma Principles in Any Organization

By Greg Brue (0-07-145548-5)

Introduces the fundamental concepts of Six Sigma and details practical steps to spearhead a Six Sigma program in the workplace.

How To Be a Great Coach: 24 Lessons for Turning on the Productivity of Every Employee

By Marshall J. Cook (0-07-143529-8)

Today's most effective coaching methods to dramatically improve the performance of your employees.

Leadership When the Heat's On: 24 Lessons in High Performance Management

By Danny Cox and John Hoover (0-07-141406-1)

Learn hands-on techniques for infusing any company with results-driven leadership at every level, especially during times of organizational turmoil.

Networking for Career Success: 24 Lessons for Getting to Know the Right People

By Diane Darling (0-07-145603-1)

Learn the steps for making mutually beneficial career connections and the know-how to cultivate those connections for the benefit of everyone involved.

Why Customers Don't Do What You Want Them To: 24 Solutions to Common Selling Problems

By Ferdinand Fournies (0-07-141750-8)

This results-focused guidebook will help you to recognize and resolve twenty common selling problems and objections and help you move beyond them.

The Powell Principles: 24 Lessons from Colin Powell, a Legendary Leader
By Oren Harari (0-07-141109-7)

Colin Powell's success as a leader is universally acknowledged. Quickly learn his approach to leadership and the methods he uses to move people and achieve goals.

Project Management: 24 Lessons to Help You Master Any Project
By Gary Heerkens (0-07-145087-4)

An overview for first-time project managers that details what is expected of him or her and how to quickly get the lay of the land.

The Welch Way: 24 Lessons from the World's Greatest CEO
By Jeffrey A. Krames (0-07-138750-1)

Quickly learn some of the winning management practices that made Jack Welch one of the most successful CEOs ever.

The Lombardi Rules: 26 Lessons from Vince Lombardi–the World's Greatest Coach
By Vince Lombardi, Jr. (0-07-141108-9)

A quick course on the rules of leadership behind Coach Vince Lombardi and how anyone can use them to achieve extraordinary results.

Making Teams Work: 24 Lessons for Working Together Successfully
By Michael Maginn (0-07-143530-1)

Guidelines for molding individual team members into a solid, functioning group.

Managing in Times of Change: 24 Tools for Managers, Individuals, and Teams
By Michael Maginn (0-07-144911-6)

Straight talk and actionable advice on making sure that any manager, team, or individual moves through change successfully.

Persuasive Proposals and Presentations: 24 Lessons for Writing Winners
By Heather Pierce (0-07-145089-0)

A short, no-nonsense approach to writing proposals and presentations that sell.

The Sales Success Handbook: 20 Lessons to Open and Close Sales Now
By Linda Richardson (0-07-141636-6)

Learn how the consultative selling approach makes everyone in the transaction a winner. Close more sales and create long-term relationships with customers.

How to Plan and Execute Strategy: 24 Steps to Implement Any Corporate Strategy Successfully
By Wallace Stettinius, D. Robley Wood, Jr., Jacqueline L. Doyle, and John L. Colley, Jr. (0-07-145604-X)

Outlines a field-proven framework to design and implement a corporate strategy that strengthens an organization's competitive advantage.

The New Manager's Handbook: 24 Lessons for Mastering Your New Role
By Morey Stettner (0-07-141334-0)

Here are 24 quick, sensible, and easy-to-implement practices to help new managers succeed from day one.

Finance for Non-Financial Managers: 24 Lessons to Understand and Evaluate Financial Health

By Katherine Wagner (0-07-145090-4)

This guide offers a bundle of lessons to clearly explain financial issues in layman's terms.

Getting Organized at Work: 24 Lessons to Set Goals, Establish Priorities, and Manage Your Time

By Ken Zeigler (0-07-145779-8)

Supplies tips, tools, ideas, and strategies for becoming more organized with work tasks and priorities in order to get more done in less time.

The Handbook for Leaders: 24 Lessons for Extraordinary Leadership

By John H. Zenger and Joseph Folkman (0-07-143532-8)

A workplace-tested prescription for encouraging the behaviors and key drivers of effective leadership, from one of today's top training teams.

Outside the USA, order multiple copies of McGraw-Hill Professional Education titles from:

Asia

McGraw-Hill Education (Asia)
Customer Service Department
60 Tuas Basin Link, Singapore 638775
Tel: (65)6863 1580
Fax: (65) 6862 3354
Email: mghasia@mcgraw-hill.com

Australia & New Zealand

McGraw-Hill Australia Pty Ltd
82 Waterloo Road
North Ryde, NSW 2113, Australia
Tel: +61-2-9900-1800
Fax: +61-2-9878-8881
Email: CService_Sydney@mcgraw-hill.com

Canada

Special Sales Representative, Trade Division
McGraw-Hill Ryerson Limited
300 Water Street
Whitby, Ontario L1N 9B6
Tel: 1-800-565-5758

Europe, Middle East, Africa

McGraw-Hill Professional, EMEA
Shoppenhangers Road, Maidenhead
Berkshire SL6 2QL, United Kingdom
Tel: +44 (0)1628 502 975
Fax: +44 (0)1628 502 167
Email: emma_gibson@mcgraw-hill.com

Other Areas

For other markets outside of the United States, e-mail Bonnie Chan at
bonnie_chan@mcgraw-hill.com.

Finance for Nonfinancial Managers
Order Form

1–99 copies	_____ copies @ $7.95 per book
100–499 copies	_____ copies @ $7.75 per book
500–999 copies	_____ copies @ $7.50 per book
1,000–2,499 copies	_____ copies @ $7.25 per book
2,500–4,999 copies	_____ copies @ $7.00 per book
5,000–9,999 copies	_____ copies @ $6.50 per book
10,000 or more copies	_____ copies @ $6.00 per book

Name _____

Title _____

Organization _____

Phone (____)_____

Street address _____

City/State (Country) _____ Zip _____

Fax (____)_____

Purchase order number (if applicable) _____

Applicable sales tax, shipping and handling will be added.

☐ VISA   ☐ MasterCard   ☐ American Express

Account number _____ Exp. date ____

Signature _____

Or call 1-800-842-3075
Corporate, Industry, & Government Sales

The McGraw-Hill Companies, Inc.
2 Penn Plaza
New York, NY 10121-2298